DATE DUE

		10/11
OCT 2 3 1999	11-1-11	
NOV 0 2 1999		
OCT 3 1 2000		
OCT 1 5 2001	WITHDRAWN	
NOV 1 3 2002		
OCT 1 2003		
NOV 1 0 2003		
NOV 0 7 2005		
NOV 1 5 2006		
NOV 1 6 2003		
DEC 1 1 2010		

GAYLORD   PRINTED IN U.S.A.

THE LITTLE WITCH'S HALLOWEEN BOOK

by Linda Glovach

Prentice-Hall, Inc., Englewood Cliffs, N.J.

Printed in the United States of America · J

Prentice-Hall International, Inc., London
Prentice-Hall of Australia, Pty. Ltd., North Sydney
Prentice-Hall of Canada, Ltd., Toronto
Prentice-Hall of India Private Ltd., New Delhi
Prentice-Hall of Japan, Inc., Tokyo

Library of Congress Cataloging in Publication Data

Glovach, Linda.
    The little witch's Halloween book.

    SUMMARY: Step-by-step instructions for a
variety of Halloween activities, foods, costumes,
and festivities.
    1. Halloween—Juvenile literature. 2. Cookery
—Juvenile literature. 3. Holiday decorations—
Juvenile literature. [1. Halloween] I. Title.
GT4965.G58   394.2′683   75-11713
ISBN 0-13-537985-7

10   9   8   7   6   5   4   3

TABLE OF CONTENTS

THE LITTLE WITCH'S CODE

1. The Little Witch shows her Halloween treats to her mother *before* she eats them.

2. The little witch and her friends stay together when they trick-or-treat. They keep an eye on the smaller children and always let an adult know where they are.

3. Halloween is a time for sharing, so the little witch collects money for charities in her Halloween costume.

4. The little witch wishes everyone a happy Halloween. Even if they don't give her a treat, she doesn't play tricks on them.

I. CARDS AND DECORATIONS

MAKING HALLOWEEN CARDS

The little witch makes her own Halloween cards. Then she puts them in special spooky envelopes and delivers or mails them to her friends in time for October 31.

SPOOKY ENVELOPE

You need: white paper, two pieces, each 6" x 10"; tape; scissors; rubber cement; black construction paper, 1 1/2" x 2".

Measure 3" in on the top edge of the white paper and make a dot. From the dot draw a curved line (to about 3" down each side) that touches the edges of the paper, to make a ghostly shape. Cut out on the lines. Near the top of the paper draw two eyes and cut them out.

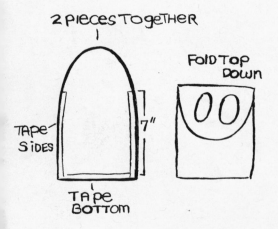

Trace this as a pattern on the other white piece of paper and cut along the lines. Tape the two pieces together 7" up each side and along the bottom. Put your card in it. Then fold the top of the envelope (untaped part) down.

8

Cut a little witch hat out of the black paper. Put a dab of rubber cement on it and stick it to the rim of the envelope to seal it closed.

When your friend opens the seal it will pop up like a full size ghost again.

HALLOWEEN FACES CARD

You need: construction paper: black, one piece, 5 1/4" x 9", and two pieces, each 1" x 2"; orange, one piece, 4 1/2" x 5 1/4"; light brown, one piece, 1" x 1 1/2"; tempera paints; scissors; glue; crayons.

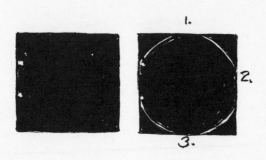

Fold width of the big black paper in half. Measure 1 1/2" in from top and bottom of the folded side and mark dots. Starting at the top dot, draw a circle to meet the other three edges of the paper, ending at the lower dot. Cut out on the lines, but not between the dots.

Glue orange circle over Black circle.

Trace the circle on the orange paper. Cut it out and glue it to the right inside of the card. Trim excess orange.

Draw a triangle on each of the 1" x 2" papers and cut them out. Glue the triangles to the cat's head for ears, as shown in the picture.

Close the card. Draw cat eyes, nose, and mouth as shown in the picture. Then cut out the eyes and the mouth. Paint the nose and whiskers. Draw triangles in the cat's eyes, and write "Happy Halloween" in the cat's mouth.

Open the card. Draw a pumpkin nose. Draw a mouth around your letters. Cut out the eyes and nose only.

Make a stem out of the brown paper by cutting a curved line on the left corner. Glue the stem 1/2" to the back of the pumpkin. The stem should be folded down when the card is closed and pulled up when the card is opened.

Write the receiver's name and your name on the inside of the front piece with a light colored pointed crayon.

Front
Of Card

11

LITTLE WITCH'S KETTLE CARD

You need: black construction paper, two pieces, 5" x 6"; 8" of string, painted black; yellow construction paper, 2 1/2" x 6 1/2"; stapler; orange tempera paint; marking pen; ruler.

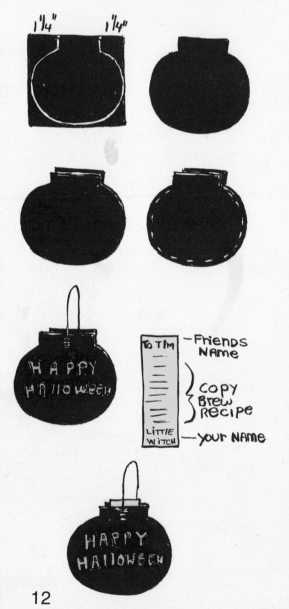

Measure 1 1/4" in from each top corner and mark a dot. From the dots draw a line 1/2" down the paper. Connect the ends of the lines together with a circle that touches the three edges of the paper. Cut along the lines.

Trace this pattern on the other piece of black paper and cut it out. Staple or tape the two pieces together along the circle part only.

Staple an end of the string to the top of each side to make a handle. Paint "Happy Halloween" on the front of the kettle. Write who the card is to on the top of the yellow strip. Then copy the Sour Grapes Brew recipe on page 46 below it, and sign your name. Slip the strip into the kettle.

12

SCARY SCARECROW

This scarecrow might make the trick-or-treaters who come to your door laugh, or it might scare them. Hang it from your doorbell or on your doorknob, so when they ring the bell or you open the door it'll wiggle.

You need: orange construction paper, two pieces, 6″ x 6″ , one piece, 5″ x 5″; heavy thread, one piece, 20″ long, two pieces, 6″ long; string, 8″ long; black construction paper, 4 1/2″ x 5″; yellow or black crepe paper, two pieces, 3″ x 4 1/2″; many yellow crepe paper strips; scissors; glue; crayon; ruler.

Make a circle out of each orange square. Start at the middle top of the 6″ x 6″ papers and draw a circle that touches the four edges of the paper. Cut out.

Copy the pattern on the right to make a witch's hat on the black paper. Cut out on the lines.

On the small 5″ circle draw pumpkin eyes, nose, and mouth. Cut them out. Glue some 1/8″ x 4″ strips of yellow crepe paper to sides and back of the pumpkin head for hair. Glue the witch's hat over it.

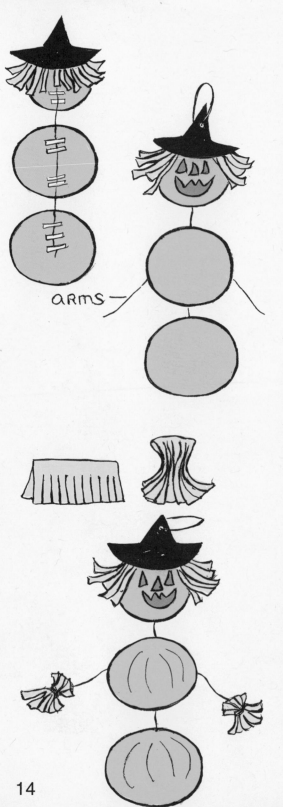

Attach the 20" thread to the back of pumpkin head with tape as shown in the picture. Come down a few inches and tape a 6" circle to the thread in two places. Attach the third circle in the same way, so all circles are evenly spaced and attached to string.

Attach 3/4" of the 6" threads to bottom sides of middle pumpkin for arms. Punch a tiny hole near top of the hat and tie the string through it to hang the scarecrow.

Fold width of the black (or yellow) crepe paper pieces in half and cut 1/8" x 1 1/2" strips up opened end. Bunch the paper together between your fingers like a witch's broom and have someone tie the end of the scarecrow's arms around the crepe paper for hands. Paint grooves on the pumpkin if you wish.

II. PARTIES AND CELEBRATIONS

PUMPKIN PATCH PARTY

The little witch likes to start the Halloween celebration with a Pumpkin Patch Party. She has it in her backyard, but you can also have it indoors, in a spacious room.

Everyone must come as a pumpkin. When you make your invitations, copy the instructions for the pumpkin costume (page 18) inside the card so your friends can make it for the party.

There is a pumpkin hunt, a cake-eating contest, and other events at the party. So start making your preparations early and be sure to send out your invitations a few days before the party.

PUMPKIN PATCH INVITATIONS

You need: orange construction paper, 7½" x 18"; light brown construction paper, 1" x 2"; scissors; pen; tempera paints; glue.

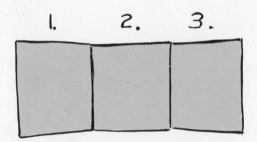

Fold the width of the orange paper in three equal parts, 6" x 7½" each. Fold the right part of the paper in. Close the card.

Mark dots 1½" in from top and bottom of left and right edges of the card. Draw curves from the dots to the top and bottom edges to form a circle. Cut out on the lines, but not between the dots. Paint on a pumpkin face.

The card opens to three parts. Write the details of the party on the left part: "To Mary: You are invited to a Pumpkin Patch Party. Where: Little Witch's House. When: Saturday afternoon. What time: 1 o'clock."

On the middle piece and right piece, starting at the top, copy the Pumpkin Costume instructions (page 18). Write: "Come as a pumpkin. Make the costume below. Then copy the directions on your card.

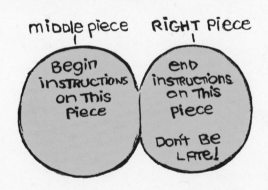

Make a stem for the pumpkin by cutting off the left corner of the brown paper in a curve. Glue it to the back of the front piece of the card.

PUMPKIN COSTUME

You need: paper grocery bag; small paper cup (3 oz. size); orange crepe paper, 20″ x 32″; orange and brown tempera paints; pencil; scissors.

Paint the bag orange. Put it over your head. If it is too long, cut some off the bottom (5 or 6 inches). Point out where your eyes, nose, and mouth are. Have someone mark the spots.

Take the bag off. Draw pumpkin eyes, nose, and mouth on the spots, big enough for your eyes, nose, and mouth to come through.

Paint the cup brown and glue it to the top center of the bag for a stem. Wear the crepe paper as a cape, fastened with a safety pin. Wear orange or brown slacks and top with brown or dark gloves.

PUMPKIN HUNT

Start the party off with a pumpkin hunt. Decorate oranges and one small pumpkin to hide before your friends come. Hide the pumpkin in a particularly tricky place.

When your friends arrive, everyone must hunt for the pumpkin until someone yells, "I found it!" The others continue to hunt until they each find an orange pumpkin head. As soon as you find something, take it and sit down at the table, until everyone is seated. But if you find an orange when you are hunting, don't pick it up until you see if you can find the pumpkin first. Everyone keeps what they find.

DECORATED ORANGES
You need: oranges, toothpicks, miniature gumdrops, colored candy dots, miniature marshmallows, candy bananas, and other candies.

Make an orange for each guest, except for the one who will find the pumpkin.

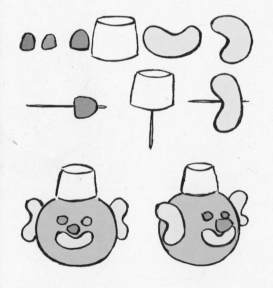

For each orange, gather two gumdrops, a dot, a marshmallow, and two candy bananas. Stick the toothpicks into the candy well enough to hold the candy on it. Then stick the long end of the toothpick into the orange to make gumdrop eyes, dot nose, marshmallow hat, banana ears and mouth.

You can make up your own candy combinations for the faces. Try to make each orange different, if you can. Put the leftover candy in little bowls to serve at the party.

DECORATED PUMPKIN
Paint eyes, nose, and mouth on the pumpkin, using three colors of your choice. Paint the stem too.

PUMPKIN CAKE-EATING CONTEST

When your friends are hungry it is time to have the cake-eating contest. Make the cake the morning of the party. The cake looks like a pumpkin.

Everyone sits around the table and admires the pumpkin cake. Then the whole cake is cut into even pieces (have your mother do it), one slice for each person. Someone says "go" and everyone has to eat their piece as fast as they can. Whoever finishes first and swallows the last crumb shouts, "Fat pumpkin!" That person is the winner and gets the prize (page 25), if she or he is not too full after all that cake.

PUMPKIN CAKE
(GINGERBREAD THAT TASTES LIKE PUMPKIN)
Mix together: 1/2 cup sugar,
                1/2 cup butter,
                1 tsp. ginger,
                1 tsp. cinnamon,
                1/2 tsp. salt.

Add one egg and beat with a fork until fluffy. Add 3/4 cup dark molasses and 3/4 cup milk. Sift 2 cups flour with 1 tsp. baking soda and add to above mixture. Bake in round pan at 325° for about 35 minutes. While cake cools, make the icing.

ICING AND DECORATIONS FOR THE CAKE

You need: 1 cup confectioner's sugar, 1 Tbsp. butter (soft) or shortening, 2 Tbsps. milk, orange food coloring, candy corn, miniature gumdrops, red hots.

Mix the sugar and butter in a bowl with a fork. Add the milk slowly. Stir until creamy. Add drops of food coloring, stirring until you get an even orange pumpkin color.

Spread the icing on the cake with a knife. Arrange some gumdrops in a triangle shape to make each eye. Arrange the candy corns in a triangle shape to make the nose. Use the red hots to outline the shape of a pumpkin's mouth on the cake.

Stick a chocolate marshmallow or a tootsie roll in the side of the top of the cake for a stem.

PRIZE FOR WINNER OF CAKE-EATING CONTEST

The winner of the cake-eating contest deserves a prize, but, oh, no, it's another pumpkin! Save some icing from the cake and ice a very large (3″) plain cookie with it.

Make a pumpkin face on it with candy corn eyes, nose, and mouth. Wrap it in an orange napkin (or paint one side of a white one) and close with tape. Tie a ribbon around it.

GHOSTLY GET-TOGETHER

On Halloween Day (October 31) the little witch has her grandest party of all. She invites her friends and tells them to wear their scariest costumes.

You can hang orange, yellow, and black balloons and crepe paper streamers along with the Little Witch's own decorations to make the room look spooky. If you have a record player, hide it out of sight (under a table or chair, or in a closet) and play scary music on it. Your friends won't know where it's coming from. The next few pages will give you some party ideas.

FLOATING FRIENDLY GHOSTS

You need: thin white paper, 20 or more pieces, each 5 1/4″ x 10″; white thread; scissors; crepe paper strips; crayons or paints; small nails; stapler.

Make ghosts: all different kinds. Mark a dot on middle top of paper.

From the dot draw curved lines to edges of paper to draw the ghost, as shown in the picture. Cut it out. Draw eyes and cut them out.

Decorate some of the ghosts. With your crayons you can make them wear eyeglasses, or have a big nose, a mustache, beard, freckles, or rosy red cheeks. Cut strips of crepe paper and glue them on for hair.

Write the name of each friend coming to the party on the back of a funny ghost.

Cut a piece of thread, about 60" or longer. Cut 6" pieces of thread and staple 1" to the back of each ghost. Hang the string up (see below) and tie each ghost to a spot on it. Try to space them out evenly.

You can hang the ghosts across the room by using longer thread and tying each end to a nail put in the wall, or you can hang them across a corner or doorway. The ghosts will look like they are floating.

TREATS TO EAT
Frosted Pumpkin and Ghost Cookies
You need: 3 dozen plain chocolate or vanilla wafers;
orange and white icings; candy corn; red hots.

Make a cup each of orange and plain white icings
(see recipe on page 24). Spread half of the amount
of wafers you have with orange and half with white
icing. Put candy corn eyes and nose and red hots for
the mouth on the orange cookies, so they look like
pumpkins. Put red hots near the top of the white
cookies for eyes, so they look like ghosts. Arrange
them on a platter and serve. Apple cider is a good
beverage to drink with these cookies.

APPLE DUNKING

If everyone wants to have a big laugh it is time to dunk for apples.

You need: a deep pan (such as a turkey roaster) or a basin; apples; blindfold.

Blindfold a player and direct him or her to the basin. Without using her hands, she must try to catch an apple with her teeth. She must keep trying until she gets one. It's not as easy as it sounds. The apples taste good with peanut butter and graham crackers.

GAMES

WICKED WITCH'S CANDY HOUSE

To play this game, choose a witch. She goes inside the house. The other players stay across the room. Then one player goes up to the house, takes a piece of candy off the roof and eats it as noisily as possible. When the witch hears this she says, "Nibble, nibble, Little Mouse, Who's that nibbling on my house?" The nibbler has to disguise her voice and say, "It's only the wind," or "I'm just a butterfly passing by," or something like that.

The witch tries to guess who it really is. She guesses once and then she runs out of the house. If she was right, the nibbler automatically becomes the next witch and goes in the house. If she was wrong, the nibbler has a chance to run away. If he makes it to the end of the line where the others are standing, he is safe and she is still the witch. If she catches him, he has to go in the house and be the new witch.

WICKED WITCH'S HOUSE
You need: an empty carton, large enough for you to fit under (from a grocery or department store); scissors; tempera paints; assorted candies; tin foil.

Turn the carton over, open end down. Draw a door on the front and a window on each side of the house. Have an adult cut out the windows and door on the lines.

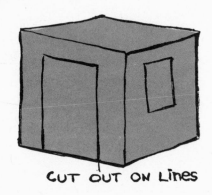

CUT OUT ON LINES

Paint the house. Paint on shutters and different candies and cookies in designs all over the house. Think of some of the cookies you like to eat for an idea, or you can copy the Halloween candy.

Put a sheet of tin foil on the top of the house and spread some candies on it, to nibble when the witch is inside the house.

GOBLIN GRAB BAG

It is nice to have a goblin grab bag at the end of the party, so your friends can take something with them when they leave.

Each person picks a surprise out of the grab bag, hoping it won't be the Spooky Booby Prize (a bag of black jelly beans). But don't worry—the Booby Prize is fun to eat too.

You need: brown grocery bag; yellow construction paper, half of a 6″ diameter circle; glue; scissors; tempera paints.

Paint the bag. Cut 4″ strips at the top and bend them down for goblin hair.

Turn the half circle into a cone. Tape the seam. Cut small flaps on the bottom. Glue the flaps to the bag for a nose.

Paint on goblin eyes and mouth. Fill the bag with the prizes and booby prize.

GOBLIN GRAB BAG PRIZES

All the bags look the same so your friends can't tell which one contains the booby prize. Make one bag, including the booby prize, for each friend.

Put about ten pieces of candy in each Halloween bag or a napkin wrapped like a bundle, then tied closed with a ribbon. Caramels, licorice, and cracker jacks are nice. Fill one bag with ten black jelly beans. Do not put jelly beans in any other bag.

When the little witch's friends walk home they trade for some of the candies they like best and the booby prize winner gets a chance to trade, too.

ALL HALLOWS' EVE

Many centuries ago, people believed that witches, goblins, ghosts, and the spirits of the deceased came back on this night to wander about.

The people, frightened by this, dressed in costumes, lit bonfires, told fortunes, and put out offerings of sweets to scare them off.

The little witch, her friends, and some of the people in her neighborhood dress in their scariest costumes and gather together for an All Hallows' Eve celebration of their own. They begin the night by lighting a small bonfire and toasting marshmallows.

GUMDROPS

ALL HALLOWS'
EVE
CELEBRATION

TOASTING MARSHMALLOWS

You can toast marshmallows outdoors, in the fireplace, or over the stove. (Dim the lights to make it spooky.)

You need: marshmallows; skewers or long forks.
Put the marshmallow on the end of the skewer and stick the tip in the flame carefully until the marshmallow is toasted the way you like it.

Apple juice or hot cider tastes good with marshmallows, and chocolate syrup sprinkled with pecans is a delicious marshmallow dip.

TELLING FORTUNES

In the past it was a custom to eat different kinds of nuts, usually with raisins, at Halloween. They are supposed to bring good luck. The Little Witch and her friends tell their fortunes with them.

You need: ten walnuts in shells; ten construction paper pieces (see colors below), each 2" x 4"; small brown paper bags; tempera paints; pen.
Look at the list below. Write the fortune that goes with the color listed below on the card of that color.

Example: on the orange card, write "Sudden fame."

Red: A dangerous journey.
Blue: A package will arrive soon.
Yellow: You will hear from an old friend.
Green: Unexpected money.
Orange: Sudden fame.
Black: An encounter with a mysterious stranger.
Purple: Someone will betray you.
White: Watch out!
Brown: You have a secret admirer.
Paint a walnut for each color listed above.

Now you are ready to play. Choose a fortune teller. She turns the cards writing side down, and puts the walnuts in the bag and shakes it well. Without looking in the bag, someone sticks his hand in it and takes out three walnuts. He looks at the colors carefully. Then the fortune teller puts them in another bag and shakes it.

This time the player picks two walnuts (without looking) out of the bag. Then he must guess what color walnut is left in the bag. If he guesses right, the fortune teller finds the card that matches the walnut left in the bag and gives it to the player. That is his fortune. If he guessed wrong, he must wait until the next round to try again. Take turns being the fortune teller. After a while you can make up some of your own fortunes, or add more walnuts and cards.

III. TRICK OR TREAT

JACK-O'-LANTERN

Probably the best fun of all at Halloween is trick or treating. Many years ago children carried jack-o'-lanterns with them when they went trick or treating. They scooped out the inside of a turnip or pumpkin, attached a string to the top, and put a candle inside. The little witch makes her jack-o'-lantern out of an orange and she takes it with her when she goes trick or treating. It can hold special candies, or it can be a decoration for your house, or a hanging pot for a plant.

You need: a large orange; string, 8″ long; tempera paints; a spoon for scooping.

Cut off the very top of the orange. Have an adult scoop out the insides of the orange thoroughly. Punch a tiny hole about 1/2″ down from the rim of the orange on each side. Tie an end of the string to each hole.

PAINT DESIGNS ON A CANDY DISH

CANDY

Set the orange aside. In a few days the skin will become hard. Then paint a pumpkin face on it. Write your name on the back.

The skin of the jack-o'-lantern will stay hard for a very long time, so be sure to save it.

BLACK CAT TRICK-OR-TREAT BAG

Some people believe that trick or treating started
centuries ago when poor people went from door
to door on Halloween day asking for cakes and fruit.

The Little Witch makes her own Halloween bag
that she carries with her to collect the goodies she
receives.

You need: grocery bag; white construction paper, 2
circles (use the rim of a soup can for size); pink
or red construction paper, 3″ x 5″; white, black, and
pink tempera paint; glue; scissors; string, 20″ long;
ruler; six straws from a broom.

Close the bag flat. Measure
5″ down from the center of
the opened end of the bag and
mark a dot. From the dot to
each open corner, draw a
curved line as in the picture.
Cut on the line, front and back
of bag together. Paint bag
black.

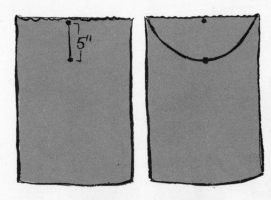

Glue on the circles for the cat's eyes and paint smaller black circles inside. Paint on a small pink nose.

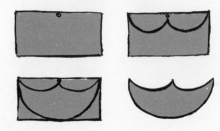

Mark a dot on the top middle of the pink paper. From the dot to each top corner, draw a curved line as in the picture. Then draw a curved line to join top corners, that touches the paper at the bottom. Cut out on the lines.

Glue it in place for the cat's mouth. Glue the broom straws next to the nose for whiskers.

Make a hole at each top corner. Put an end of a string through each corner and tie in a knot to make a handle.

LITTLE WITCH'S SPECIAL TRICK-OR-TREAT SURPRISES

The little witch likes to give her friends something special when they come trick or treating. So, she surprises them with her own little trick or treat bundles.

You need: orange or white paper napkins; circles of orange construction paper (use the rim of a soup can for size); black construction paper, 3″ x 3″; glue; scissors; paint; string; candy.

Put some candy (about ten or more pieces) on the paper napkin. Fold up the edges, and tie the napkin closed with a piece of string.

Paint a pumpkin face on each circle. Draw a witch's hat on the black paper as shown in the picture and cut it out. Glue either a pumpkin or a hat to the front of each napkin.

HALLOWEEN NIGHT AT HOME

After the parties and the trick or treating the little witch and her family like to spend a quiet evening at home. Some of her closest friends join them and they all sit in front of the fireplace to have refreshments and tell some of the spookiest stories you ever heard. The little witch brews a special punch to serve with chocolate witch wafers.

LITTLE WITCH'S SOUR GRAPES BREW
(SERVES 8 to 10)

You need: 3 cups apple juice, 2 cups grape juice, two oranges, a lemon, and honey or sugar to sweeten.

Mix the liquids together, including the juice of one orange. Squeeze some lemon juice into it. Start with 2 tablespoons of honey or sugar to sweeten. Add more if you like. Serve in a punch bowl, with orange slices floating on top.

WITCH WAFERS

You need: plain chocolate wafers; 1/2 cup honey; 1/2 cup whipped cream; two bowls or cups; a platter.

Put the honey in one small bowl and fill another with the whipped cream. Put the cookies around the bowls on the platter. Dip the wafers in the honey or the cream or both and eat!

Grandfather Witch starts off the evening with a very spooky story.

Index

R